THE MEDITERRANEAN DIET COOKBOOK FOR TWO

Quick, Easy, and Flavorful Recipes to Enjoy Every Day

MIRA GREEN

TABLE OF CONTENTS

INTRODUCTION TO THE MEDITERRANEAN DIET COOKBOOK FOR TWO

Welcome to the world of the Mediterranean diet, where simplicity, freshness, and flavor come together in harmony to create the perfect meals for two. This book is designed for those who value healthy eating and aim to improve their quality of life through a well-balanced diet.

The Mediterranean diet, recognized as one of the healthiest in the world, is based on the traditional eating habits of Mediterranean countries such as Greece, Italy, and Spain. It emphasizes abundant fresh vegetables and fruits, whole grains, nuts, seeds, olive oil, fish, and seafood. The cornerstones of this diet are avoiding processed foods and sweets and consuming meat and dairy products in moderation.

This book is specially crafted for couples who want to enjoy delicious and nutritious meals together. Inside, you'll find various recipes, each designed for two servings, that are easy to prepare at home. Every recipe has been carefully selected, from breakfasts and appetizers to main courses and desserts, to offer balanced nutrition and every meal's joy.

This book will become your reliable guide to Mediterranean cuisine and inspire you to culinary experiments. May each dish bring you and your partner joy and health, and may the time spent together preparing and savoring food become even more precious.

Bon appétit and good health!

CHAPTER 1:
WHAT IS THE MEDITERRANEAN DIET, AND WHAT DOES IT INCLUDE

The traditional cuisine and eating customs of people in Mediterranean nations, including Greece, Italy, Spain, and southern France, serve as the foundation for the Mediterranean diet. This diet is widely regarded as one of the world's healthiest and most balanced, thanks to its numerous health benefits.

Key Principles of the Mediterranean Diet

1. **Abundance of Vegetables and Fruits**: Vegetables and fruits form the foundation of the Mediterranean diet. Because of their high content of vitamins, minerals, antioxidants, and fiber, they improve general health and lower the risk of chronic illnesses.

2. **Whole Grains**: Bread, pasta, rice, and other grain products are preferably consumed in whole grain form. These foods are high in fiber and complex carbohydrates, providing long-lasting satiety and stable energy levels.

3. **Olive Oil**: Olive oil is the primary source of fat in the Mediterranean diet. It is rich in monounsaturated fats and antioxidants, which help lower "bad" cholesterol levels and protect the heart.

4. **Nuts and Seeds**: Nuts and seeds are excellent sources of protein, healthy fats, and micronutrients. They help support cardiovascular health and provide long-lasting satiety.

5. **Fish and Seafood**: Fish and seafood, especially fatty varieties like salmon, sardines, and mackerel, are rich in omega-3 fatty acids, which benefit the heart and brain.

6. **Moderate Consumption of Dairy Products**: The Mediterranean diet allows for moderate consumption of dairy products, preferably yogurt and cheese. They are sources of calcium and probiotics, which support bone health and the digestive system.

7. **Limited Red Meat Consumption**: Red meat and processed meat products are consumed in limited quantities. Instead, preference is given to poultry, fish, and plant-based protein sources.

8. **Minimal Sugar and Processed Foods**: The Mediterranean diet excludes or minimizes the consumption of sugar and processed foods, such as fast food, sugary drinks, and ready-made meals.

Other Important Aspects

Apart from dietary selections, the Mediterranean diet has significant lifestyle elements. Regular exercise, sharing meals with loved ones, and consuming wine—mostly red—in moderation during meals are important components.

Health Benefits

Studies have indicated that a Mediterranean diet may lower the risk of neurological disorders, type 2 diabetes, heart disease, and several types of cancer. It also enhances general health and aids in maintaining a healthy weight.

By following the principles of the Mediterranean diet, you can enjoy delicious and diverse food while taking care of your health and well-being.

CHAPTER 2 : BREAKFAST

GREEK YOGURT WITH FRUITS AND NUTS

Serving Size: 2
Prep Time: 10 minutes

Nutrition Information (per serving):

- Calories: ~300 kcal
- Protein: ~15g
- Carbohydrates: ~35g
- Fat: ~10g
- Fiber: ~5g

Ingredients:

- 2 cups Greek yogurt
- 1 cup fresh fruit (e.g., strawberries, blueberries, peaches)
- 1/4 cup nuts (e.g., almonds, walnuts)
- Honey to taste

Directions:

1. Prepare the Yogurt:

- Divide the Greek yogurt evenly into two bowls.

2. Add the Fruit:

- Wash and slice the fresh fruit.
- Evenly distribute the fruit over the yogurt in each bowl.

3. Add the Nuts:

- Roughly chop the nuts if desired.
- Sprinkle the nuts over the fruit and yogurt.

4. Sweeten:

- Drizzle honey over the top to taste.

5. Serve:

- Mix slightly if desired and serve immediately.

Enjoy a healthy and delicious Mediterranean breakfast!

OATMEAL WITH FRUITS AND HONEY

Servings: 2
Prep Time: 10 minutes
Cook Time: 10 minutes

Ingredients:

- 1 cup (90 g) rolled oats
- 2 cups (480 ml) milk (or any plant-based milk)
- 1 tablespoon honey
- 1/2 teaspoon cinnamon
- 1/2 teaspoon vanilla extract
- 1 small apple, diced
- 1/2 cup (75 g) berries (such as blueberries, strawberries, or raspberries)
- A pinch of salt

Directions:

1. Prepare the Oats:

- Combine the rolled oats, milk, and a pinch of salt in a medium saucepan. Bring to a boil over medium-high heat, stirring occasionally.

2. Cook the Oats:

- Once it boils, reduce the heat to a simmer and cook, stirring occasionally, for 5 to 7 minutes or until the oats are soft and most of the milk has been absorbed.

3. Add Flavor:

- Stir in the honey, cinnamon, and vanilla extract. Mix well to combine.

4. Add Fruits:

- Gently fold in the diced apple and berries. Cook for another 1-2 minutes to warm the fruits.

5. Serve:

- Divide the oatmeal between two bowls. Drizzle with extra honey if desired, and garnish with additional fruit or a sprinkle of cinnamon if you like.

Nutrition Info (per serving):

- **Calories:** 290
- **Protein:** 10 g
- **Carbohydrates:** 50 g
- **Fiber:** 6 g
- **Sugar:** 20 g
- **Fat:** 6 g
- **Saturated Fat:** 2 g

VEGETABLE OMELETTE

Servings: 2
Prep Time: 10 minutes
Cook Time: 10 minutes

Ingredients:

- 4 large eggs
- 1/4 cup (60 ml) milk
- 1 tablespoon olive oil or butter
- 1/2 cup (75 g) bell peppers, diced
- 1/2 cup (75 g) tomatoes, diced
- 1/2 cup (75 g) spinach, chopped
- 1/4 cup (30 g) onions, finely chopped
- 1/4 cup (30 g) shredded cheese (optional)
- Salt and pepper to taste
- Fresh herbs for garnish (optional)

Directions:

1. Prepare the Vegetables:

- Heat the olive oil or butter in a nonstick pan over medium heat. Add the onions and sauté for two to three minutes or until transparent.
- Cook for a further two minutes after adding the bell peppers. When the spinach has wilted, add the tomatoes and simmer, seasoning with a little salt and pepper. After taking the veggies out of the skillet, set them aside.

2. Prepare the Egg Mixture:

- Whisk the eggs, milk, salt, and pepper in a bowl until well combined.

3. Cook the Omelette:

- Wipe the skillet clean and heat more olive oil or butter over medium heat. Transfer the egg mixture to the skillet and cook, uncovered, until the edges begin to firm, about 2 minutes.
- Tilt the skillet and gently raise the edges with a spatula to allow any raw eggs to ooze to the edges. Cook for another 1-2 minutes until the eggs are mostly set.

4. Add the Vegetables:

- Spread the cooked vegetables evenly over one-half of the omelet. Sprinkle with shredded cheese if desired.

5. Fold and Serve:

- Carefully fold the omelet in half over the filling. Allow the omelet to continue cooking and the cheese to melt by cooking for an additional minute.
- Transfer the omelet to a platter, and if you like, top with fresh herbs.

Nutrition Info (per serving):

- **Calories:** 290
- **Protein:** 17 g
- **Carbohydrates:** 10 g
- **Fiber:** 2 g
- **Sugar:** 6 g
- **Fat:** 20 g
- **Saturated Fat:** 6 g

AVOCADO TOAST WITH POACHED EGG

Servings: 2
Prep Time: 10 minutes
Cook Time: 10 minutes

Ingredients:

- 2 slices of whole-grain bread
- 1 ripe avocado
- 1 tablespoon lemon juice
- 1/4 teaspoon salt
- 1/4 teaspoon black pepper
- 2 large eggs
- 1 tablespoon white vinegar (optional, helps with poaching)
- Red pepper flakes (optional, for garnish)
- Fresh herbs (garnish with parsley or cilantro, if desired)

Directions:

1. Prepare the Avocado Spread:

- Mash the ripe avocado with a fork in a bowl. Stir in the black pepper, salt, and lemon juice. Adjust seasoning to taste.

2. Toast the Bread:

- Toast the slices of bread to your desired level of crispness using a toaster or under a broiler.

3. Poach the Eggs:

- Fill a medium saucepan with two to three inches of water, then simmer it slowly over medium heat. Add the white vinegar if using.
- Crack one egg into a small bowl. Gently place the egg into the water that is simmering. Repeat this with the second egg if poaching both at the same time.
- Cook the eggs for 3-4 minutes until the whites are set but the yolks are still runny. The eggs may be taken out of the water and drained on paper towels using a slotted spoon.

4. Assemble the Toast:

- Spread the mashed avocado evenly over the toasted bread slices.
- Top each slice of avocado toast with a poached egg.

5. Garnish and Serve:

- Sprinkle with red pepper flakes and fresh herbs if desired. Serve immediately.

Nutrition Info (per serving):

- **Calories:** 320
- **Protein:** 14 g
- **Carbohydrates:** 32 g
- **Fiber:** 8 g
- **Sugar:** 2 g
- **Fat:** 18 g
- **Saturated Fat:** 3 g

BERRY AND SPINACH SMOOTHIE

Servings: 2
Prep Time: 5 minutes

Ingredients:

- 1 cup (150 g) mixed berries (fresh or frozen, such as strawberries, blueberries, and raspberries)
- 1 cup (30 g) fresh spinach leaves
- 1 banana
- 1/2 cup (120 ml) Greek yogurt (plain or vanilla)
- Half a cup (120 ml) of almond milk (or any other type of milk you choose)
- For sweetness, add one tablespoon of honey or maple syrup.
- Ice cubes, if desired, for a smoothie that is colder

Directions:

1. Prepare the Ingredients:
- If using fresh berries, wash them thoroughly. If using frozen berries, there's no need to thaw them. Peel the banana.

2. Blend:
- Combine the mixed berries, fresh spinach, banana, Greek yogurt, and almond milk in a blender.
- You may taste and add honey or maple syrup for a sweeter smoothie.

- Process until smooth. A little extra milk can be added if the smoothie is too thick. Blend again after adding a few ice cubes if you want it cooler.

3. Serve:

- Transfer the smoothie into glasses, then serve right away.

Nutrition Info (per serving):

- **Calories:** 220
- **Protein:** 8 g
- **Carbohydrates:** 32 g
- **Fiber:** 6 g
- **Sugar:** 20 g
- **Fat:** 6 g
- **Saturated Fat:** 1 g

CLASSIC FRITTATA FOR TWO

Servings: 2
Prep Time: 10 minutes
Cook Time: 20 minutes

Ingredients:

- 4 large eggs
- 1/4 cup (60 ml) milk or cream
- 1/2 cup (75 g) shredded cheese (such as cheddar, mozzarella, or feta)
- 1/2 cup (75 g) diced bell peppers (any color)
- 1/4 cup (30 g) diced onions
- 1/2 cup (75 g) cherry tomatoes, halved
- 1/2 cup (75 g) spinach leaves
- 1 tablespoon olive oil
- Salt and pepper to taste
- Fresh herbs (optional, such as basil or parsley for garnish)

Directions:

1. Prepare the Oven and Ingredients:

- Set the oven temperature to 375°F, or 190°C.
- In a bowl, whisk together the eggs, milk or cream, salt, and pepper. Add the cheese shreds and stir.

2. Cook the Vegetables:

- In an oven-safe skillet (10 inches or smaller), preheat the olive oil over medium heat. Add the diced onions and sauté for 3–4 minutes or until they are transparent.
- Cook the chopped bell peppers for two to three minutes or until they become tender.
- Stir in the cherry tomatoes and spinach, cooking until the spinach is wilted.

3. Add the Egg Mixture:

- Cover the veggies in the skillet with the egg mixture. Stir gently to distribute the ingredients evenly.

4. Cook the Frittata:

- Cook the frittata over medium heat for approximately five minutes or until the edges begin to firm.
- Transfer the skillet to the preheated oven and bake for 10-15 minutes until the frittata is set and the top is golden brown.

5. Serve:

- Take it out of the oven and let it cool for a few minutes. Garnish with fresh herbs if desired. Slice into wedges and serve.

Nutrition Info (per serving):

- **Calories:** 320
- **Protein:** 18 g
- **Carbohydrates:** 10 g
- **Fiber:** 3 g
- **Sugar:** 6 g
- **Fat:** 22 g
- **Saturated Fat:** 8 g

CLASSIC SPANISH TORTILLA

Servings: 2
Prep Time: 10 minutes
Cook Time: 20 minutes

Ingredients:

- 2 large potatoes (about 1/2 lb or 225 g), peeled and thinly sliced
- 1 small onion, thinly sliced (optional)
- 4 large eggs
- 1/4 cup (60 ml) olive oil
- Salt and black pepper to taste

Directions:

1. Prepare the Potatoes:

- Heat the olive oil in a nonstick pan over medium heat.
- Add the thinly sliced potatoes (and onion) to the skillet. Add salt and pepper to taste. Cook, tossing occasionally, until the potatoes are soft and beginning to turn golden, about 15 to 20 minutes.

2. Prepare the Egg Mixture:

- While the potatoes cook, beat the eggs in a bowl—season with salt and pepper.

3. Combine Potatoes and Eggs:

- After the potatoes are cooked, remove them from the oil and combine them with the beaten eggs in the basin. Stir to combine, ensuring the potatoes are well coated with the egg mixture.

4. Cook the Tortilla:

- Wipe the skillet clean and add a little more olive oil. Heat over medium heat.
- Fill the skillet with the potato and egg mixture. Cook for about 5 minutes or until the bottom is set and golden brown.
- Carefully flip the tortilla using a plate or a large spatula. Cook the other side for another 4-5 minutes until fully set and golden brown.

5. Serve:

- Before slicing, slide the tortilla onto a platter and let it cool for a few minutes. Serve warm or at room temperature.

Nutrition Info (per serving):

- **Calories:** 340
- **Protein:** 14 g
- **Carbohydrates:** 30 g
- **Fiber:** 4 g
- **Sugar:** 3 g
- **Fat:** 20 g
- **Saturated Fat:** 4 g

CLASSIC POLENTA

Servings: 2
Prep Time: 10 minutes
Cook Time: 30 minutes

Ingredients:

- 1 cup (200 g) polenta (cornmeal)
- 4 cups (960 ml) water or vegetable broth
- 2 tablespoons olive oil or butter
- 50 grams, or 1/2 cup, grated Parmesan cheese (optional)
- Salt and black pepper to taste

Directions:

1. Prepare the Liquid:

- Heat a big saucepan over high heat and add the water or vegetable broth. If preferred, add a small sprinkle of salt.

2. Add the Polenta:

- Gradually whisk in the polenta to prevent lumps from forming. Reduce the heat to low.

3. Cook the Polenta:

- Cook the polenta for another 25 to 30 minutes, or until it thickens and pulls away from the pan's sides, stirring it often with a wooden spoon.

4. Finish and Serve:

- If using, stir in the olive oil or butter and grated Parmesan cheese. Adjust seasoning with salt and black pepper.
- Serve hot, or let it cool slightly and cut into slices or squares. Polenta can also be grilled or baked after it has cooled and set.

Nutrition Info (per serving):

- **Calories:** 180
- **Protein:** 5 g
- **Carbohydrates:** 30 g
- **Fiber:** 2 g
- **Sugar:** 1 g
- **Fat:** 4 g
- **Saturated Fat:** 1 g

SPANISH-STYLE FRITTATA FOR TWO

Servings: 2
Prep Time: 10 minutes
Cook Time: 20 minutes

Ingredients:

- 4 large eggs
- 1/4 cup (60 ml) milk
- 1/2 cup (75 g) potatoes, peeled and thinly sliced
- 1/4 cup (30 g) onion, finely chopped
- 1/4 cup (75 g) bell peppers, diced (red, green, or yellow)
- 1/4 cup (30 g) cherry tomatoes, halved
- 1/4 cup (30 g) Spanish chorizo or ham, diced (optional)
- 1/4 cup (30 g) grated Manchego cheese (or any cheese of your choice)
- 2 tablespoons olive oil
- Salt and black pepper to taste
- Fresh herbs for garnish (optional, such as parsley)

Directions:

1. Prepare the Vegetables:

- Heat a single tablespoon of olive oil in a medium oven-safe pan over medium heat.
- Add the thinly sliced potatoes and cook, stirring occasionally, until they are tender and lightly golden, about 10 minutes. Remove and set aside.

2. Cook the Other Vegetables:

- In the same skillet, add another tablespoon of olive oil. Sauté the chopped onion and bell peppers until softened, about 3-4 minutes.

- Cook for a further two minutes after adding the cherry tomatoes. If using, add the diced chorizo or ham and cook for an additional 2 minutes.

3. Prepare the Egg Mixture:

- Whisk together the eggs, milk, salt, and black pepper.

3. Combine and Cook:

- Return the cooked potatoes to the skillet with the other vegetables. Stir to combine.
- Pour the egg mixture over the vegetables and boil for about 5 to 7 minutes or until the edges start to get firm.
- Evenly distribute the grated cheese on top.

4. Finish Cooking:

- Place the pan in the oven that has been prepared, and bake for ten to fifteen minutes, or until the frittata is set through and the top is browned.

5. Serve:

- Let the frittata cool slightly before slicing. If preferred, garnish with fresh herbs and serve warm.

Nutrition Info (per serving):

- **Calories:** 320
- **Protein:** 16 g
- **Carbohydrates:** 20 g
- **Fiber:** 3 g
- **Sugar:** 4 g
- **Fat:** 21 g
- **Saturated Fat:** 7 g

SWEET POTATO WITH CHICKEN AND EGG FOR TWO

Servings: 2
Prep Time: 15 minutes
Cook Time: 30 minutes

Ingredients:

- 2 medium sweet potatoes
- 2 boneless, skinless chicken breasts
- 2 large eggs
- 1 tablespoon olive oil
- 1 teaspoon smoked paprika
- 1/2 teaspoon garlic powder
- 1/2 teaspoon onion powder
- Salt and pepper to taste
- Fresh parsley or cilantro for garnish (optional)

Directions:

1. Prepare the Sweet Potatoes:

- Preheat your oven to 400°F (200°C).
- Cut the sweet potatoes into 1-inch cubes after peeling them. Add the salt, pepper, and half a tablespoon of olive oil.

- Distribute the sweet potato cubes on a baking pan in a single layer. Roast, rotating the pan halfway through, for about 20 minutes, or until the sweet potatoes are soft and beginning to caramelize.

2. Cook the Chicken:

- Season the chicken breasts with smoked paprika, garlic powder, onion powder, salt, and pepper.
- Heat the remaining 1/2 tablespoon of olive oil in a skillet over medium heat. When the chicken reaches an internal temperature of 165°F (74°C), add the chicken breasts and cook for 5 to 7 minutes on each side.
- Take off the chicken from the skillet, let it rest for a few minutes, and then cut it into strips.

3. Cook the Eggs:

- In the same skillet used for the chicken, cook the eggs to your preference—season with salt and pepper. You can fry, scramble, or poach them.

4. Assemble the Dish:

- Divide the roasted sweet potatoes between two plates. Top with sliced chicken and a cooked egg.
- Garnish with fresh parsley or cilantro.

Nutrition Info (per serving):

- **Calories:** 400
- **Protein:** 30 g
- **Carbohydrates:** 35 g
- **Fiber:** 6 g
- **Sugar:** 8 g
- **Fat:** 15 g
- **Saturated Fat:** 2 g

BAKED APPLES WITH PEANUT BUTTER AND JAM

Servings: 2
Prep Time: 10 minutes
Cook Time: 25 minutes

Ingredients:

- 2 large apples (such as Honeycrisp or Fuji)
- 2 tablespoons peanut butter (smooth or chunky)
- 2 tablespoons fruit jam or jelly (such as strawberry, raspberry, or apricot)
- 1 tablespoon honey (optional for extra sweetness)
- 1/2 teaspoon cinnamon
- 1/4 cup (30 g) granola or chopped nuts (optional for topping)

Directions:

1. Prepare the Apples:

- Preheat your oven to 350°F (175°C).
- Wash the apples and remove the cores using an apple core or a knife. If you don't have an apple core, you can cut the apples into rings and remove the core from each ring.

2. Stuff the Apples:

- Mix the peanut butter with the jam or jelly in a small bowl until well combined. If desired, add honey for extra sweetness.

- Spoon the peanut butter and jam mixture into the center of each apple, packing it in as much as possible.

3. Season and Bake:

- Sprinkle the cinnamon over the stuffed apples.
- Place the apples in a baking dish. Add a little water to the bottom of the dish to help keep the apples moist during baking.
- Bake for about 25 minutes, or until the apples are soft but retain their form, in a preheated oven.

4. Serve:

- Take the apples out of the oven and give them a little time to cool.
- If desired, top with granola or chopped nuts for added crunch.

Nutrition Info (per serving, without additional toppings):

- **Calories:** 220
- **Protein:** 4 g
- **Carbohydrates:** 32 g
- **Fiber:** 5 g
- **Sugar:** 22 g
- **Fat:** 10 g
- **Saturated Fat:** 2 g

COUSCOUS WITH STRAWBERRIES FOR TWO

Servings: 2
Prep Time: 10 minutes
Cook Time: 5 minutes

Ingredients:

- 1 cup (150 g) couscous
- 1 cup (240 ml) water
- 1 tablespoon honey or maple syrup
- 1/2 teaspoon vanilla extract
- 1 cup (150 g) fresh strawberries, hulled and sliced
- 2 tablespoons chopped nuts (optional, such as almonds or pistachios)
- Fresh mint leaves for garnish (optional)

Directions:

1. Prepare the Couscous:

- Place one cup of water in a medium pot and heat to a boil. Take off the heat.
- Stir in the couscous, cover the saucepan, and let it sit for about 5 minutes to allow the couscous to absorb the water and become tender.
- Fill a medium saucepan with one cup of water and bring it to a boil. Turn off the heat.

2. Prepare the Strawberries:

- While the couscous is resting, slice the strawberries.

3. Assemble the Dish:
- Divide the couscous between two bowls. Top with sliced strawberries.
- If desired, sprinkle with chopped nuts for added crunch.

4. Garnish and Serve:
- Garnish with fresh mint leaves if desired. Serve immediately.

Nutrition Info (per serving):
- **Calories:** 230
- **Protein:** 5 g
- **Carbohydrates:** 44 g
- **Fiber:** 3 g
- **Sugar:** 22 g
- **Fat:** 3 g
- **Saturated Fat:** 0.5 g

GREEN KIWI AND APPLE SMOOTHIE

Servings: 2
Prep Time: 5 minutes

Ingredients:

- Two sliced and peeled kiwis
- One large apple, cored and sliced (you may use any kind you choose).1 cup (30 g) fresh spinach leaves
- 1/2 cup (120 ml) Greek yogurt (plain or vanilla)
- One-half cup (120 ml) of water or apple juice
- For sweetness, add one tablespoon of honey or maple syrup, if preferred.
- Ice cubes (optional for a colder smoothie)

Directions:

1. Prepare the Ingredients:

- Peel and slice the kiwis. Core and slice the apple. Wash the spinach leaves.

2. Blend:

- Combine the sliced kiwis, apple, spinach leaves, Greek yogurt, and apple juice or water in a blender.
- You may taste and add honey or maple syrup for a sweeter smoothie.
- Blend until smooth. If you like colder, add a few ice cubes and blend again.

3. Serve:

- Pour the smoothie into glasses.

Nutrition Info (per serving):

- **Calories:** 200
- **Protein:** 8 g
- **Carbohydrates:** 35 g
- **Fiber:** 5 g
- **Sugar:** 22 g
- **Fat:** 4 g
- **Saturated Fat:** 2 g

TOAST WITH SMOKED SALMON, AVOCADO, AND POACHED EGG

Servings: 2
Prep Time: 10 minutes
Cook Time: 10 minutes

Ingredients:

- 2 slices of whole-grain or sourdough bread
- 1 ripe avocado
- 1 tablespoon lemon juice
- Salt and pepper to taste
- 2 oz (60 g) smoked salmon
- 2 large eggs
- 1 tablespoon white vinegar (optional, helps with poaching)
- Fresh dill or chives for garnish (optional)

Directions:

1. Prepare the Avocado Spread:
- Mash the ripe avocado with a fork. Add the pepper, salt, and lemon juice and stir. Taste and adjust the seasoning.

2. Toast the Bread:
- Toast the slices of bread to your desired level of crispness using a toaster or under a broiler.

31

3. Poach the Eggs:

- Fill a medium saucepan with two to three inches of water, then simmer it slowly over medium heat. If using white vinegar, add it now.
- Crack one egg into a small bowl. Drop the egg into the heating water. Repeat this with the second egg if poaching both at the same time.
- Cook the eggs for 3-4 minutes until the whites are set but the yolks are still runny. The eggs may be taken out of the water and drained on paper towels using a slotted spoon.

4. Assemble the Toast:

- Spread the mashed avocado evenly over the toasted bread slices.
- Place slices of smoked salmon on top of each piece.
- Place a poached egg on top of each slice of toast.

5. Garnish and Serve:

- If preferred, garnish with fresh chives or dill. Serve right away.

Nutrition Info (per serving):

- **Calories:** 320
- **Protein:** 17 g
- **Carbohydrates:** 27 g
- **Fiber:** 6 g
- **Sugar:** 2 g
- **Fat:** 17 g
- **Saturated Fat:** 3 g

CHAPTER 3 : SALADS

BURRATA CHEESE AND TOMATO SALAD

Servings: 2
Prep Time: 10 minutes

Ingredients:

- 1 large burrata cheese ball (about 4 oz/115 g)
- 2 cups (300 g) cherry tomatoes, halved
- 1 cup (50 g) arugula or fresh basil leaves
- 2 tablespoons extra-virgin olive oil
- 1 tablespoon balsamic vinegar
- 1/2 teaspoon honey
- Salt and pepper to taste
- Fresh basil or parsley for garnish (optional)

Directions:

1. Prepare the Salad:

- Combine the halved cherry tomatoes and arugula or basil leaves in a large bowl.

2. Make the Dressing:

- In a small dish or container, thoroughly mix the olive oil, balsamic vinegar, honey, salt, and pepper.

3. Assemble the Salad:

- Drizzle the dressing over the tomato and arugula mixture. Toss gently to coat.

4. Add the Burrata:

- Carefully place the burrata cheese in the center of the salad. You can leave it whole or tear it into pieces for easier serving.

5. Garnish and Serve:

- If preferred, garnish with fresh parsley or basil. Serve right away.

Nutrition Info (per serving):

- **Calories:** 300
- **Protein:** 10 g
- **Carbohydrates:** 8 g
- **Fiber:** 2 g
- **Sugar:** 5 g
- **Fat:** 25 g
- **Saturated Fat:** 10 g

FETA CHEESE AND TOMATO SALAD

Servings: 2
Prep Time: 10 minutes

Ingredients:

- 2 cups (300 g) cherry tomatoes, halved
- 1/2 cup (75 g) crumbled feta cheese
- 1/4 cup (30 g) red onion, thinly sliced
- 1/4 cup (30 g) black or Kalamata olives, pitted and halved (optional)
- 2 tablespoons extra-virgin olive oil
- 1 tablespoon red wine vinegar
- 1/2 teaspoon dried oregano
- Salt and pepper to taste
- Fresh basil or parsley for garnish (optional)

Directions:

1. Prepare the Ingredients:

- Wash and halve the cherry tomatoes. Thinly slice the red onion. If using, pit and halve the olives.

2. Assemble the Salad:

- Combine the cherry tomatoes, feta cheese crumbles, chopped red onion, and olives (if using) in a big bowl.

3. Make the Dressing:

- Combine the olive oil, red wine vinegar, dried oregano, salt, and pepper.

4. Dress the Salad:

- Drizzle the dressing over the tomato and feta mixture. Toss gently to coat.

5. Garnish and Serve:

- If preferred, garnish with fresh parsley or basil. Serve right away.

Nutrition Info (per serving):

- **Calories:** 220
- **Protein:** 8 g
- **Carbohydrates:** 12 g
- **Fiber:** 3 g
- **Sugar:** 6 g
- **Fat:** 17 g
- **Saturated Fat:** 6 g

GREEK SALAD

Servings: 2
Prep Time: 10 minutes

Ingredients:

- 1 cup (150 g) cherry tomatoes, halved
- 1/2 cucumber, sliced
- 1/4 red onion, thinly sliced
- 1/4 cup (30 g) Kalamata olives
- 1/4 cup (30 g) crumbled feta cheese
- 2 tablespoons extra-virgin olive oil
- 1 tablespoon red wine vinegar
- 1/2 teaspoon dried oregano
- Salt and pepper to taste

Directions:

1. Combine a bowl of tomatoes, cucumber, red onion, olives, and feta cheese.
2. Whisk together olive oil, vinegar, vinegar, oregano, salt, and pepper in a small bowl.
3. Drizzle dressing over salad and toss gently.

Nutrition Info (per serving):

- **Calories:** 200
- **Protein:** 8 g
- **Carbohydrates:** 12 g

- **Fiber:** 3 g
- **Sugar:** 6 g
- **Fat:** 16 g
- **Saturated Fat:** 6 g

TOMATO AND CUCUMBER SALAD

Servings: 2
Prep Time: 10 minutes

Ingredients:

- 1 cup (150 g) cherry tomatoes, halved
- 1/2 cucumber, sliced
- 1/4 cup (30 g) red onion, thinly sliced
- 2 tablespoons extra-virgin olive oil
- 1 tablespoon lemon juice
- Salt and pepper to taste
- Fresh dill for garnish (optional)

Directions:

1. In a bowl, mix the tomatoes, cucumber, and red onion.
2. In a small bowl, combine lemon juice, olive oil, salt, and pepper. Pour dressing over salad and toss gently. Garnish with dill if desired.

Nutrition Info (per serving):

- **Calories:** 150
- **Protein:** 2 g
- **Carbohydrates:** 12 g
- **Fiber:** 3 g
- **Sugar:** 6 g
- **Fat:** 11 g
- **Saturated Fat:** 1.5 g

CHICKPEA AND SPINACH SALAD

Servings: 2
Prep Time: 10 minutes

Ingredients:

- 1 cup (150 g) cooked chickpeas
- 2 cups (60 g) fresh spinach
- 1/4 cup (30 g) diced red bell pepper
- 1/4 cup (30 g) diced cucumber
- 2 tablespoons extra-virgin olive oil
- 1 tablespoon lemon juice
- 1/2 teaspoon ground cumin
- Salt and pepper to taste

Directions:

1. Combine chickpeas, spinach, bell pepper, and cucumber in a bowl.
2. Whisk together olive oil, lemon juice, cumin, salt, and pepper in a small bowl.
3. Drizzle dressing over salad and toss gently.

Nutrition Info (per serving):

- **Calories:** 250
- **Protein:** 10 g
- **Carbohydrates:** 30 g
- **Fiber:** 8 g

- **Sugar:** 6 g
- **Fat:** 10 g
- **Saturated Fat:** 1.5 g

ROASTED RED PEPPER AND FETA SALAD

Servings: 2
Prep Time: 15 minutes

Ingredients:

- 1 cup (150 g) roasted red peppers, sliced
- 1/4 cup (30 g) crumbled feta cheese
- 1/4 cup (30 g) black olives, sliced
- 2 cups (60 g) mixed greens
- 2 tablespoons extra-virgin olive oil
- 1 tablespoon balsamic vinegar
- Salt and pepper to taste

Directions:

1. Combine roasted red peppers, feta cheese, olives, and mixed greens in a bowl.
2. Mix olive oil, balsamic vinegar, salt, and pepper in a small bowl.
3. Drizzle dressing over salad and toss gently.

Nutrition Info (per serving):

- **Calories:** 220
- **Protein:** 8 g
- **Carbohydrates:** 10 g
- **Fiber:** 3 g
- **Sugar:** 5 g
- **Fat:** 18 g
- **Saturated Fat:** 5 g

MEDITERRANEAN QUINOA SALAD

Servings: 2
Prep Time: 15 minutes

Ingredients:

- 1 cup (185 g) cooked quinoa
- 1/2 cup (75 g) cherry tomatoes, halved
- 1/4 cup (30 g) diced cucumber
- 1/4 cup (30 g) Kalamata olives, halved
- 1/4 cup (30 g) crumbled feta cheese
- 2 tablespoons extra-virgin olive oil
- 1 tablespoon lemon juice
- Salt and pepper to taste

Directions:

1. Combine cooked quinoa, cherry tomatoes, cucumber, olives, and feta cheese in a bowl.
2. In a small bowl, combine olive oil, lemon juice, salt, and pepper.
3. Drizzle dressing over salad and toss gently.

Nutrition Info (per serving):

- **Calories:** 300
- **Protein:** 10 g
- **Carbohydrates:** 40 g
- **Fiber:** 5 g

- **Sugar:** 6 g
- **Fat:** 12 g
- **Saturated Fat:** 3 g

CUCUMBER, TOMATO, AND AVOCADO SALAD

Servings: 2
Prep Time: 10 minutes

Ingredients:

- 1/2 cucumber, diced
- 1 cup (150 g) cherry tomatoes, halved
- 1 ripe avocado, diced
- 2 tablespoons extra-virgin olive oil
- 1 tablespoon lemon juice
- Salt and pepper to taste
- Fresh basil or parsley for garnish (optional)

Directions:

1. Combine cucumber, cherry tomatoes, and avocado in a bowl.
2. You can mix olive oil, lemon juice, salt, and pepper in a small bowl.
3. Drizzle dressing over salad and toss gently. Garnish with basil or parsley if desired.

Nutrition Info (per serving):

- **Calories:** 290
- **Protein:** 3 g
- **Carbohydrates:** 20 g
- **Fiber:** 7 g
- **Sugar:** 5 g
- **Fat:** 25 g
- **Saturated Fat:** 3.5 g

BEET AND GOAT CHEESE SALAD

Servings: 2
Prep Time: 15 minutes

Ingredients:

- 1 cup (150 g) cooked beets, sliced
- 1/4 cup (30 g) goat cheese, crumbled
- 1/4 cup (30 g) walnuts, chopped
- 2 cups (60 g) mixed greens
- 2 tablespoons extra-virgin olive oil
- 1 tablespoon balsamic vinegar
- Salt and pepper to taste

Directions:

1. Combine beets, goat cheese, walnuts, and mixed greens in a bowl.
2. Mix olive oil, balsamic vinegar, salt, and pepper in a small bowl.
3. Drizzle dressing over salad and toss gently.

Nutrition Info (per serving):

- **Calories:** 290
- **Protein:** 8 g
- **Carbohydrates:** 25 g

- **Fiber:** 5 g
- **Sugar:** 10 g
- **Fat:** 20 g
- **Saturated Fat:** 5 g

COUSCOUS SALAD WITH FRESH CUCUMBERS, SWEET PEPPERS, AND OLIVES

Servings: 2
Prep Time: 15 minutes
Cook Time: 5 minutes

Ingredients:

- 1 cup (150 g) couscous
- 1 cup (240 ml) water
- 1/2 cup (75 g) cucumber, diced
- 1/2 cup (75 g) sweet bell pepper, diced (any color)
- 1/4 cup (30 g) black or Kalamata olives, pitted and sliced
- 2 tablespoons fresh parsley, chopped
- 2 tablespoons extra-virgin olive oil
- 1 tablespoon lemon juice
- 1/2 teaspoon dried oregano
- Salt and pepper to taste

Directions:

1. Prepare the Couscous:

- Place one cup of water in a medium pot and heat to a boil. Remove from heat.
- Stir in the couscous, cover, and let it sit for about 5 minutes until it is tender and has absorbed the water.
- Use a fork to fluff the couscous and let it cool slightly.

2. Prepare the Vegetables:

- While the couscous is cooling, dice the cucumber and bell pepper and slice the olives.
- Chop the fresh parsley.

3. Assemble the Salad:

- Combine the cooked couscous, diced cucumber, bell pepper, olives, and chopped parsley in a large bowl.

4. Make the Dressing:

- Whisk the olive oil, lemon juice, dried oregano, salt, and pepper in a small bowl.

5. Dress the Salad:

- Pour the dressing over the combination of couscous and toss lightly to incorporate.

6. Serve:

- Serve the salad and enjoy it.

Nutrition Info (per serving):

- **Calories:** 250
- **Protein:** 6 g
- **Carbohydrates:** 32 g
- **Fiber:** 4 g
- **Sugar:** 5 g
- **Fat:** 12 g
- **Saturated Fat:** 1.5 g

CHAPTER 4 :
MAIN DISHES

GRILLED DORADO FOR TWO

Servings: 2
Prep Time: 15 minutes
Cook Time: 20 minutes

Ingredients:

- 2 dorado fish (about 8-10 oz each), cleaned and gutted
- 2 tablespoons olive oil
- 2 cloves garlic, minced
- 1 lemon, sliced
- To taste, add salt and pepper
- Add 1 tablespoon of fresh thyme leaves.
- Fresh parsley for garnish (optional)

Directions:

1. Preheat the Grill:

- Preheat your grill to medium-high heat. If using a charcoal grill, let the coals burn until they are covered with white ash.

2. Prepare the Fish:

- Rinse the dorado fish under cold water and pat dry with paper towels.
- Rub the inside and outside of each fish with olive oil. Season generously with salt and pepper.
- Stuff the cavity of each fish with minced garlic, lemon slices, and thyme.

3. Grill the Fish:

- Place the fish on the grill grates. Grill for about 8-10 minutes per side, depending on the thickness of the fish. The fish is done when the flesh is opaque and flakes easily with a fork. Avoid overcooking to keep the fish tender and moist.

4. Serve:

- Take the fish from the grill and give it some time to rest.
- Garnish with fresh parsley if desired.

Nutrition Info (per serving):

- **Calories:** 250
- **Protein:** 30 g
- **Carbohydrates:** 1 g
- **Fiber:** 0 g
- **Sugar:** 0 g
- **Fat:** 14 g
- **Saturated Fat:** 2 g

GAZPACHO WITH ROASTED VEGETABLES

Servings: 2
Prep Time: 20 minutes
Cook Time: 25 minutes

Ingredients:

For the Gazpacho:

- 4 large ripe tomatoes, peeled and chopped
- 1/2 cucumber, peeled and chopped
- 1/2 red bell pepper, chopped
- 1/4 red onion, chopped
- 2 cloves garlic, minced
- 2 tablespoons extra-virgin olive oil
- 2 tablespoons red wine vinegar
- 1/2 teaspoon ground cumin
- Salt and pepper to taste

For the Roasted Vegetables:

- 1/2 red bell pepper, sliced
- 1/2 zucchini, sliced
- 1/2 red onion, sliced
- 1 tablespoon olive oil
- 1/2 teaspoon dried oregano

- Salt and pepper to taste

Directions:

1. Roast the Vegetables:
- Preheat your oven to 400°F (200°C).
- Arrange the sliced red bell pepper, zucchini, and red onion on a baking sheet.
- Drizzle with olive oil, then season with salt, pepper, and dried oregano.
- Bake the veggies for 20 to 25 minutes or until they are soft and starting to caramelize.
- Allow to cool slightly.

2. Prepare the Gazpacho:
- In a blender or food processor, combine the tomatoes, cucumber, red bell pepper, red onion, and garlic.
- Process until smooth.
- Include salt, pepper, ground cumin, red wine vinegar, and olive oil. Toss to blend again.
- Adjust seasoning to taste.

3. Chill the Gazpacho:
- To cool and let the flavors mingle, transfer the gazpacho to a bowl or pitcher and place it in the refrigerator for at least an hour.

4. Serve:
- Serve the chilled gazpacho in bowls with the roasted vegetables on top or on the side as a garnish.

Nutrition Info (per serving):
- **Calories:** 150
- **Protein:** 3 g
- **Carbohydrates:** 20 g
- **Fiber:** 5 g
- **Sugar:** 10 g
- **Fat:** 7 g
- **Saturated Fat:** 1 g

PAELLA WITH MUSSELS

Servings: 2
Prep Time: 15 minutes
Cook Time: 30 minutes

Ingredients:

- 1 cup (200 g) short-grain paella rice or Arborio rice
- 1 cup (240 ml) chicken or vegetable broth
- 1/2 cup (120 ml) white wine
- 1/2 cup (75 g) onion, finely chopped
- 2 cloves garlic, minced
- 1/2 cup (75 g) red bell pepper, diced
- 1/2 cup (75 g) green peas (fresh or frozen)
- 1/2 cup (75 g) diced tomatoes (canned or fresh)
- 1/2 teaspoon smoked paprika
- 1/4 teaspoon saffron threads (optional)
- 1 tablespoon extra-virgin olive oil
- 1 cup (150 g) mussels, cleaned and debearded
- Salt and pepper to taste
- Fresh parsley for garnish (optional)
- Lemon wedges for serving (optional)

Directions:

1. Prepare the Ingredients:

- Clean and debeard the mussels. Discard any that are open and do not close when tapped.

2. Cook the Base:

- Heat the Italian olive oil in a large skillet or paella pan over medium heat.
- Add the onion and garlic, and cook for three to four minutes or until softened.
- Add the red bell pepper and cook for another 2 minutes.
- Stir in the diced tomatoes, smoked paprika, and saffron threads (if using). Cook for 2 minutes.

3. Add the Rice:

- Heat the lovely olive oil in a large skillet or paella pan over medium heat.

4. Add Liquids and Cook:

- Pour in the white wine and cook until it has mostly evaporated.
- Add the broth, either vegetable or chicken and heat until it boils.
- Lower the heat to a simmer, cover, and cook the rice for approximately fifteen minutes or until it is almost done.

5. Add Mussels and Peas:

- Gently stir in the mussels and green peas.
- Cover and cook for another 5-7 minutes until the mussels have opened and the rice is fully cooked. Discard any mussels that do not open.

6. Finish and Serve:

- Remove from heat and let it sit for a few minutes before serving.
- Garnish with fresh parsley and lemon wedges.

Nutrition Info (per serving):

- **Calories:** 400
- **Protein:** 20 g
- **Carbohydrates:** 50 g
- **Fiber:** 5 g
- **Sugar:** 6 g
- **Fat:** 12 g
- **Saturated Fat:** 2 g

SQUID WITH FETA AND OLIVES

Servings: 2
Prep Time: 15 minutes
Cook Time: 10 minutes

Ingredients:

- 8 oz (225 g) squid, cleaned and sliced into rings
- 1 tablespoon extra-virgin olive oil
- 2 cloves garlic, minced
- 1/2 cup (75 g) cherry tomatoes, halved
- 1/4 cup (30 g) black or Kalamata olives, pitted and sliced
- 1/4 cup (30 g) crumbled feta cheese
- 1 tablespoon fresh parsley, chopped
- 1 tablespoon lemon juice
- Salt and pepper to taste

Directions:

1. Prepare the Squid:
- Rinse the squid rings under cold water and pat dry with paper towels.

2. Cook the Squid:
- Heat the olive oil in a big pan over medium-high heat.

- Add the minced garlic and sauté until fragrant, about 30 seconds.
- Add the squid rings to the skillet and cook, turning regularly, for two to three minutes or until they become opaque and are cooked through. Be careful not to overcook, as squid can become burdensome.

3. Add Vegetables:
- Add the cherry tomatoes and simmer, stirring, until they become soft, about 2 minutes.
- Add the olives and cook for 1-2 minutes.

4. Finish and Serve:
- Remove the pan from the heat and add the crumbled feta cheese.
- Season with salt and pepper to taste and drizzle with lemon juice. Garnish with fresh parsley and serve immediately.

Nutrition Info (per serving):
- **Calories:** 270
- **Protein:** 20 g
- **Carbohydrates:** 7 g
- **Fiber:** 2 g
- **Sugar:** 4 g
- **Fat:** 20 g
- **Saturated Fat:** 6 g

CHICKEN AND TURMERIC PAELLA

Servings: 2
Prep Time: 15 minutes
Cook Time: 30 minutes

Ingredients:

- 1 cup (200 g) short-grain paella rice or Arborio rice
- 1 cup (240 ml) chicken broth
- 1/2 cup (120 ml) white wine
- 1/2 pound (225 g) chicken thighs, boneless and skinless, cut into bite-sized pieces
- 1/2 cup (75 g) onion, finely chopped
- 2 cloves garlic, minced
- Diced red bell pepper, 1/2 cup (75 g)
- 1/2 cup (75 g) green peas (fresh or frozen)
- 1/2 cup (75 g) diced tomatoes (canned or fresh)
- 1 teaspoon ground turmeric
- 1/2 teaspoon smoked paprika
- 1/2 teaspoon dried thyme
- 1 tablespoon extra-virgin olive oil
- Salt and pepper to taste

- Fresh parsley for garnish (optional)
- Lemon wedges for serving (optional)

Directions:

1. Prepare the Chicken:
- Sprinkle salt and pepper on the chicken pieces.

2. Cook the Chicken:
- Heat the olive oil in a large skillet or paella pan over medium heat.
- Cook for a further five to seven minutes or until the chicken pieces are browned on all sides. Take the chicken from the skillet and place it aside.

3. Cook the Base:
- Add the onion you diced to the same skillet and cook it for three to four minutes or until it becomes tender.
- Cook for a further minute after adding the minced garlic and stirring.
- After adding the chopped red bell pepper, simmer for an additional two minutes.

4. Add Spices and Rice:
- Stir in the ground turmeric, smoked paprika, and dried thyme.
- Add the paella rice and simmer for one to two minutes, until it starts to softly toast.

5. Add Liquids and Cook:
- Pour in the white wine and cook until it has mostly evaporated.
- Stir in the chicken stock and shredded tomatoes. Heat till boiling.
- Reduce heat to low, return the chicken to the skillet, and cover. Simmer for about 15 minutes or until the rice is nearly cooked through.

6. Add Peas:
- Cook for five minutes, or until the rice and chicken are well cooked, after stirring in the green peas.

7. Finish and Serve:
- Remove from heat and let it sit for a few minutes before serving.
- Garnish with fresh parsley and lemon wedges if desired.

Nutrition Info (per serving):
- **Calories:** 400
- **Protein:** 30 g

- **Carbohydrates:** 45 g
- **Fiber:** 5 g
- **Sugar:** 6 g
- **Fat:** 10 g
- **Saturated Fat:** 2 g

GRILLED VEAL CHOPS

Servings: 2
Prep Time: 15 minutes
Cook Time: 10-12 minutes

Ingredients:

- 2 veal chops (about 8 oz each)
- 2 tablespoons extra-virgin olive oil
- 2 cloves garlic, minced
- One tablespoon of chopped fresh rosemary (or one teaspoon of dried rosemary)
- 1 teaspoon dried thyme, or 1 tablespoon chopped fresh thyme
- 1 tablespoon lemon juice
- Salt and pepper to taste
- Lemon wedges for serving (optional)
- Fresh parsley for garnish (optional)

Directions:

1. Marinate the Veal Chops:

- Combine the olive oil, minced garlic, rosemary, thyme, and lemon juice in a small bowl.
- Add salt and pepper to season the veal chops.

- Rub the marinade mixture over the veal chops, making sure they are well coated.
- Cover and refrigerate for at least 30 minutes to marinate (up to 2 hours for more flavor).

2. Preheat the Grill:

- Preheat your grill to medium-high heat. If using a charcoal grill, let the coals burn until they are covered with white ash.

3. Grill the Veal Chops:

- Take the veal chops out of the marinade and let the extra fall off.
- Place the veal chops on the grill. Grill for about 5-6 minutes per side or until the chops are cooked to your desired level of doneness. For medium-rare, the internal temperature should be about 145°F (63°C).

4. Rest and Serve:

- Remove the veal chops from the grill and let them rest for a few minutes before serving.
- Garnish with fresh parsley and serve with lemon wedges if desired.

Nutrition Info (per serving):

- **Calories:** 320
- **Protein:** 30 g
- **Carbohydrates:** 1 g
- **Fiber:** 0 g
- **Sugar:** 0 g
- **Fat:** 22 g
- **Saturated Fat:** 8 g

CANNELLONI WITH SPINACH AND CHEESE

Servings: 2
Prep Time: 20 minutes
Cook Time: 30 minutes

Ingredients:

- 8-10 cannelloni tubes
- 1 cup (225 g) ricotta cheese
- 1 cup (100 g) fresh spinach, chopped
- 50 grams, or 1/2 cup, grated Parmesan cheese
- 1 cup (100 g) shredded mozzarella cheese
- 1/2 cup (120 ml) marinara sauce
- 1/4 cup (60 ml) heavy cream
- 1 egg
- 1/4 teaspoon nutmeg
- Salt and pepper to taste
- Fresh basil or parsley for garnish (optional)

Directions:

1. Preheat the Oven:

- Preheat your oven to 375°F (190°C).

2. Cook the Cannelloni:

- Cook the cannelloni tubes as directed on the box or until al dente in a large saucepan of boiling salted water. Drain and rinse under cold water to prevent sticking.

3. Prepare the Filling:

- In a medium bowl, mix together the ricotta cheese, Parmesan cheese, chopped spinach, egg, nutmeg, salt, and pepper. Mix well until thoroughly combined.

4. Stuff the Cannelloni:

- Carefully fill each cannelloni tube with the spinach and cheese mixture. You can use a piping bag or a small spoon to do this.

5. Prepare the Baking Dish:

- Line the bottom of a baking dish with half of the marinara sauce.
- Arrange the stuffed cannelloni tubes in the baking dish in a single layer.

6. Add Sauce and Cream:

- Cover the cannelloni with the leftover marinara sauce.
- Evenly drizzle the top with the heavy cream.

7. Add Cheese and Bake:

- Sprinkle with the shredded mozzarella cheese.
- Bake the baking dish for 20 minutes in the oven, covered with aluminum foil.
- Take off the foil and bake the cheese for ten minutes or until it turns brown and bubbling.

8. Serve:

- Let the cannelloni cool slightly before serving.
- Garnish with fresh basil or parsley if desired.

Nutrition Info (per serving):

- **Calories:** 500
- **Protein:** 25 g
- **Carbohydrates:** 50 g
- **Fiber:** 3 g
- **Sugar:** 6 g
- **Fat:** 25 g
- **Saturated Fat:** 14 g

CANNELLONI WITH SPINACH AND SHRIMP IN BECHAMEL SAUCE

Servings: 2
Prep Time: 30 minutes
Cook Time: 30 minutes

Ingredients:

For the Cannelloni Filling:

- 8-10 cannelloni tubes
- 1 cup (200 g) fresh spinach, chopped
- 1 cup (200 g) cooked shrimp, chopped
- 1/2 cup (50 g) ricotta cheese
- 30 grams, or 1/4 cup, grated Parmesan cheese
- 1 tablespoon olive oil
- 1 small onion, finely chopped
- 1 clove garlic, minced
- Salt and pepper to taste

For the Bechamel Sauce:

- 2 tablespoons butter
- 2 tablespoons all-purpose flour
- 1 1/2 cups (360 ml) milk
- 50 grams, or 1/2 cup, grated Parmesan cheese

- 1/4 teaspoon ground nutmeg
- Salt and pepper to taste

Directions:

1. Preheat the Oven:
- Preheat your oven to 375°F (190°C).

2. Cook the Cannelloni:
- Cook the cannelloni tubes as directed on the box or until al dente in a large saucepan of boiling salted water. Drain and rinse under cold water to prevent sticking.

3. Prepare the Filling:
- Heat olive oil in a skillet over medium heat.
- Add the chopped onion and cook until softened about 3-4 minutes.
- Cook for a further minute after adding the minced garlic.
- Cook the chopped spinach until it wilts after adding it. Take off the heat and allow to cool a little.
- Combine the spinach mixture, Parmesan cheese, ricotta cheese, and chopped shrimp in a bowl; add salt and pepper to taste.

4. Prepare the Bechamel Sauce:
- In a small saucepan over medium heat, melt the butter.
- To make a roux, add the flour and whisk continuously for one to two minutes.
- Gradually whisk in the milk, ensuring there are no lumps.
- Continue cooking and whisking until the sauce thickens, about 5 minutes.
- Turn off the heat and mix in the nutmeg, salt, pepper, and grated Parmesan cheese.

5. Stuff the Cannelloni:
- Carefully fill each cannelloni tube with the spinach and shrimp mixture using a piping bag or a small spoon.

6. Assemble the Dish:
- Line a baking dish's bottom with a thin coating of bechamel sauce.
- Layer the filled cannelloni tubes in the dish one at a time.
- Drizzle the cannelloni with the leftover bechamel sauce.

7. Bake:
- Bake the baking dish in the oven for 20 minutes with the foil covering it.
- Take off the foil and bake for ten minutes, or until the top is yellow-brown and the sauce is bubbling.

Serve:

- Let the cannelloni cool slightly before serving.

Nutrition Info (per serving):

- **Calories:** 600
- **Protein:** 35 g
- **Carbohydrates:** 45 g
- **Fiber:** 3 g
- **Sugar:** 8 g
- **Fat:** 30 g
- **Saturated Fat:** 15 g

EGGPLANT PARMESAN

Servings: 2
Prep Time: 30 minutes
Cook Time: 45 minutes

Ingredients:

- 1 large eggplant
- 1/2 cup (60 g) all-purpose flour
- 2 large eggs
- 1 cup (100 g) breadcrumbs (preferably Italian-seasoned)
- 50 grams, or 1/2 cup, grated Parmesan cheese
- 1 cup (240 ml) marinara sauce
- 1 cup (100 g) shredded mozzarella cheese
- 1/4 cup (30 g) fresh basil leaves, chopped (plus extra for garnish)
- 1/4 cup (60 ml) olive oil
- Salt and pepper to taste

Directions:

1. Prepare the Eggplant:

- Slice the eggplant into 1/4-inch thick rounds.
- To remove extra moisture, sprinkle the slices with salt on both sides and let them set for 20 minutes. Rinse and pat dry with paper towels.

2. Bread the Eggplant:

- Assemble three shallow dishes for breading: one should include flour, another should have beaten eggs, and a third should contain a mixture of breadcrumbs and grated Parmesan cheese.
- Coat each eggplant slice in the breadcrumb mixture, pressing lightly to adhere, after dredging it in flour and dipping it in beaten eggs.

3. Fry the Eggplant:

- In a big skillet, warm up the olive oil over medium heat.
- Fry the breaded eggplant slices in batches for two to three minutes on each side or until golden brown and crispy. Add more oil to the skillet as needed. Drain on paper towels.

4. Assemble the Dish:

- Preheat your oven to 375°F (190°C).
- Line the bottom of a baking dish with a thin layer of marinara sauce.
- Arrange a layer of fried eggplant slices over the sauce.
- Spoon marinara sauce over the eggplant, then sprinkle with shredded mozzarella cheese and chopped basil.
- Continue layering until all the ingredients are utilized, then top with a thick layer of mozzarella cheese and marinara sauce.

5. Bake:

- Bake the baking dish for 20 minutes in the oven, covered with aluminum foil.
- Take off the foil and bake the cheese for ten to fifteen minutes or until it becomes brown and bubbling.

6. Serve:

- Let the eggplant parmesan cool for a few minutes before garnishing with additional fresh basil. Serve warm.

Nutrition Info (per serving):

- **Calories:** 450
- **Protein:** 20 g
- **Carbohydrates:** 40 g
- **Fiber:** 8 g
- **Sugar:** 10 g
- **Fat:** 25 g
- **Saturated Fat:** 8 g

FILET MIGNON STEAK

Servings: 2
Prep Time: 15 minutes
Cook Time: 15 minutes

Ingredients:

- 2 filet mignon steaks (about 6-8 oz each)
- 2 tablespoons olive oil
- Salt and black pepper to taste
- 2 cloves garlic, minced
- One tablespoon of freshly chopped thyme or rosemary (optional)
- 2 tablespoons butter
- 1/4 cup (60 ml) red wine (optional for deglazing)
- 1/4 cup (60 ml) beef broth (optional for deglazing)

Directions:

1. Prepare the Steaks:

- Take the steaks out of the fridge and give them about half an hour to come to room temperature.
- With paper towels, pat the steaks dry to get rid of any remaining moisture.
- Liberally season the steaks on both sides with salt and black pepper.

2. Preheat the Skillet:

- In a pan, heat the olive oil over medium-high heat until it shimmers.

3. Sear the Steaks:

- Add the steaks to the heated pan and cook until medium-rare, 3 to 4 minutes per side. To get the required level of doneness, adjust the cooking time:
- **Rare:** 2-3 minutes per side
- **Medium-Rare:** 3-4 minutes per side
- **Medium:** 4-5 minutes per side
- **Medium-Well:** 5-6 minutes per side
- **Well-Done:** 6-7 minutes per side
- Add minced garlic and fresh rosemary or thyme (if using) to the skillet during the last minute of cooking.

4. Add Butter:

- During the last minute of cooking, add the butter to the skillet and spoon the melted butter over the steaks for added flavor.

5. Rest the Steaks:

- Take the steaks out of the skillet and allow them to rest for about five minutes on a platter with a loose foil cover. This facilitates the redistribution of the fluids.

6. Make the Pan Sauce (Optional):

- Add red wine and beef broth to the skillet, if preferred, and scrape off any browned pieces from the pan's bottom. Reduce by half by simmering for 3–4 minutes over medium heat. Before serving, spoon the sauce over the steaks.

7. Serve:

- Serve the filet mignon steaks with your favorite sides, and enjoy!

Nutrition Info (per serving, based on medium-rare):

- **Calories:** 350
- **Protein:** 30 g
- **Carbohydrates:** 0 g
- **Fiber:** 0 g
- **Sugar:** 0 g
- **Fat:** 25 g
- **Saturated Fat:** 10 g

MEDITERRANEAN CHICKEN SKEWERS

Servings: 2
Prep Time: 20 minutes (plus marinating time)
Cook Time: 10-12 minutes

Ingredients:

- 2 chicken breasts, cut into cubes
- 2 tablespoons olive oil
- 1 tablespoon lemon juice
- 1 teaspoon dried oregano
- 1 teaspoon garlic powder
- Salt and pepper to taste
- Fresh parsley, chopped (for garnish)

Directions:

1. Marinate the Chicken:

- Combine olive oil, lemon juice, oregano, garlic powder, salt, and pepper in a bowl.
- Add chicken cubes and toss to coat. Marinate for at least 30 minutes.

2. Prepare and Cook:

- Thread the marinated chicken onto skewers.
- Turn the heat up to medium-high on the grill or grill pan.
- Cook the chicken on the skewers for 10 to 12 minutes, rotating them once or until the chicken is well-cooked and has nice grill marks.

3. Serve:

- Garnish with chopped parsley and serve it.

Nutrition Info (per serving):

- **Calories:** 250
- **Protein:** 30 g
- **Carbohydrates:** 1 g
- **Fiber:** 0 g
- **Sugar:** 0 g
- **Fat:** 14 g
- **Saturated Fat:** 2 g

BEEF STUFFED BELL PEPPERS

Servings: 2
Prep Time: 20 minutes
Cook Time: 30 minutes

Ingredients:

- 2 large bell peppers, tops cut off and seeds removed
- 1/2 pound (225 g) ground beef
- 1/2 cup (75 g) cooked quinoa
- 1/2 cup (100 g) diced tomatoes
- 1/4 cup (25 g) diced onion
- 1 clove garlic, minced
- 1 teaspoon dried basil
- Salt and pepper to taste
- 1/4 cup (30 g) shredded mozzarella cheese (optional)

Directions:

1. Prepare the Filling:
- Brown the ground beef in a pan over medium heat. Drain excess fat.
- Add onion, garlic, and diced tomatoes. Cook until onions are soft.
- Stir in cooked quinoa, basil, salt, and pepper.

2. Stuff the Peppers:
- Preheat oven to 375°F (190°C).

- Stuff the meat mixture into each bell pepper. Place peppers in a baking dish. Sprinkle with shredded mozzarella if desired.

3. Bake:

- Bake peppers for 25 to 30 minutes or until they are soft.

Nutrition Info (per serving):

- **Calories:** 300
- **Protein:** 25 g
- **Carbohydrates:** 20 g
- **Fiber:** 5 g
- **Sugar:** 6 g
- **Fat:** 15 g
- **Saturated Fat:** 6 g

LAMB CHOPS WITH MINT AND GARLIC

Servings: 2
Prep Time: 15 minutes (plus marinating time)
Cook Time: 10-12 minutes

Ingredients:

- 4 lamb chops
- 2 tablespoons olive oil
- 2 cloves garlic, minced
- 2 tablespoons fresh mint, chopped
- 1 tablespoon lemon juice
- Salt and pepper to taste

Directions:

1. Marinate the Lamb:

- In a bowl, combine olive oil, garlic, mint, lemon juice, salt, and pepper.
- Rub the mixture over the lamb chops and marinate for 30 minutes.

2. Cook the Lamb:

- Turn the heat up to medium-high level on the grill or grill pan.
- Grill lamb chops to the desired doneness, about 4–5 minutes on each side for medium-rare.

3. Serve:

- Let lamb chops rest for a few minutes before serving.

Nutrition Info (per serving):

- **Calories:** 400
- **Protein:** 30 g
- **Carbohydrates:** 0 g
- **Fiber:** 0 g
- **Sugar:** 0 g
- **Fat:** 30 g
- **Saturated Fat:** 12 g

MEDITERRANEAN STUFFED CHICKEN

Servings: 2
Prep Time: 20 minutes
Cook Time: 30 minutes

Ingredients:

- 2 chicken breasts
- 1/2 cup (75 g) sun-dried tomatoes, chopped
- 1/4 cup (30 g) feta cheese, crumbled
- 1/4 cup (30 g) black olives, chopped
- 1 tablespoon olive oil
- 1 teaspoon dried oregano
- Salt and pepper to taste

Directions:

1. Prepare the Filling:

- In a bowl, mix sun-dried tomatoes, feta cheese, and olives.

2. Stuff the Chicken:

- Preheat oven to 375°F (190°C).
- Cut a pocket into each chicken breast and stuff with the filling mixture.
- Secure openings with toothpicks and season with salt, pepper, and oregano.

3. Cook the Chicken:

- In an oven-safe skillet, warm the olive oil over medium-high heat.
- Sear chicken breasts for 2-3 minutes per side until golden brown.
- Place skillet in oven; bake until chicken is done, 20 to 25 minutes.

Nutrition Info (per serving):

- **Calories:** 350
- **Protein:** 35 g
- **Carbohydrates:** 5 g
- **Fiber:** 1 g
- **Sugar:** 2 g
- **Fat:** 20 g
- **Saturated Fat:** 7 g

GREEK BEEF KEBABS

Servings: 2
Prep Time: 20 minutes (plus marinating time)
Cook Time: 10-12 minutes

Ingredients:

- 1/2 pound (225 g) beef sirloin, cut into cubes
- 2 tablespoons olive oil
- 1 tablespoon lemon juice
- 1 teaspoon dried oregano
- 1 teaspoon ground cumin
- 2 cloves garlic, minced
- Salt and pepper to taste
- Fresh mint for garnish (optional)

Directions:

1. Marinate the Beef:

- Add olive oil, lemon juice, oregano, cumin, garlic, salt, and pepper in a bowl.
- Add beef cubes and toss to coat. Marinate for at least 30 minutes.

2. Prepare and Cook:

- Thread marinated beef onto skewers.
- Turn the heat up to medium-high on the grill or grill pan. Grill skewers for 10-12 minutes, turning occasionally, until beef is cooked to your desired doneness.

3. Serve:

- If required, garnish with fresh mint and serve with Greek salad on the side.

Nutrition Info (per serving):

- **Calories:** 300
- **Protein:** 30 g
- **Carbohydrates:** 2 g
- **Fiber:** 1 g
- **Sugar:** 1 g
- **Fat:** 20 g
- **Saturated Fat:** 7 g

MEDITERRANEAN SHRIMP AND QUINOA

Servings: 2
Prep Time: 10 minutes
Cook Time: 20 minutes

Ingredients:

- 1 cup (185 g) quinoa
- 1 1/2 cups (360 ml) water or vegetable broth
- 1 tablespoon olive oil
- 1/2 pound (225 g) shrimp, peeled and deveined
- 1 clove garlic, minced
- 1/2 cup (75 g) cherry tomatoes, halved
- 1/4 cup (30 g) Kalamata olives, sliced
- 1/4 cup (30 g) crumbled feta cheese
- 1 tablespoon fresh parsley, chopped
- Salt and pepper to taste

Directions:

1. Cook the Quinoa:

- Rinse quinoa under cold water. Quinoa should be combined with broth or water in a saucepan. When the liquid is absorbed, about 15 minutes after bringing it to a boil, lower the heat to low, cover, and simmer; fluff with a fork.

2. Prepare the Shrimp:

- Heat olive oil in a skillet over medium heat. Add garlic and cook for 1 minute.

- Add shrimp and cook for three to four minutes on each side or until pink and opaque.

3. Combine and Serve:
- Toss quinoa with cherry tomatoes, olives, and feta cheese—season with salt and pepper.
- Serve shrimp on top of the quinoa mixture, garnished with fresh parsley.

Nutrition Info (per serving):
- **Calories:** 400
- **Protein:** 30 g
- **Carbohydrates:** 40 g
- **Fiber:** 5 g
- **Sugar:** 6 g
- **Fat:** 15 g
- **Saturated Fat:** 3 g

LEMON GARLIC BAKED COD

Servings: 2
Prep Time: 10 minutes
Cook Time: 15-20 minutes

Ingredients:

- 2 cod fillets (about 6 oz each)
- 2 tablespoons olive oil
- 2 cloves garlic, minced
- 1 lemon, sliced
- 1 tablespoon fresh thyme, chopped
- Salt and pepper to taste
- Lemon wedges for serving

Directions:

1. Prepare the Cod:

- Preheat oven to 400°F (200°C). Place cod fillets on a baking sheet.
- Spray with olive oil, then season with salt, pepper, thyme, and chopped garlic. Place slivers of lemon over the fillets.

2. Bake:

- Bake in the oven for 15-20 minutes or until the cod is flaky and cooked through.

3. Serve:

- Serve with lemon wedges on the side.

Nutrition Info (per serving):

- **Calories:** 250
- **Protein:** 30 g
- **Carbohydrates:** 1 g
- **Fiber:** 0 g
- **Sugar:** 0 g
- **Fat:** 15 g
- **Saturated Fat:** 2 g

GRILLED SALMON WITH HERBS

Servings: 2
Prep Time: 10 minutes
Cook Time: 10 minutes

Ingredients:

- 2 salmon fillets (about 6 oz each)
- 2 tablespoons olive oil
- 1 tablespoon fresh dill, chopped
- 1 tablespoon fresh parsley, chopped
- 1 lemon, zest and juice
- Salt and pepper to taste

Directions:

1. Prepare the Salmon:

- Turn the heat up to medium-high on the grill. Salmon fillets are seasoned with salt, pepper, lemon zest, dill, and parsley after being brushed with olive oil.

2. Grill the Salmon:

- Grill salmon for 4-5 minutes per side or until it flakes easily with a fork.

3. Serve:

- Serve with a squeeze of lemon juice.

Nutrition Info (per serving):

- **Calories:** 350
- **Protein:** 30 g
- **Carbohydrates:** 0 g
- **Fiber:** 0 g
- **Sugar:** 0 g
- **Fat:** 25 g
- **Saturated Fat:** 4 g

SHRIMP AND VEGGIE STIR-FRY

Servings: 2
Prep Time: 15 minutes
Cook Time: 10 minutes

Ingredients:

- 1/2 pound (225 g) shrimp, peeled and deveined
- 1 tablespoon olive oil
- 1 bell pepper, sliced
- 1 cup (100 g) snap peas
- 1 cup (100 g) cherry tomatoes, halved
- 2 cloves garlic, minced
- Two tablespoons soy sauce (or tamari for gluten-free)
- 1 tablespoon lemon juice
- 1 teaspoon fresh ginger, minced
- Salt and pepper to taste

Directions:

1. Cook the Shrimp:
- In a big skillet, warm up the olive oil over medium-high heat.
- Cook the ginger and garlic together for one minute.

- Add the shrimp and cook for 3–4 minutes or until they are pink and opaque. Take out of the skillet and place aside.

2. Stir-Fry the Vegetables:
- Add bell pepper, snap peas, and cherry tomatoes to the same skillet.
- Stir-fry the vegetables for 3–4 minutes or until they are crisp-tender.

3. Combine and Serve:
- Return shrimp to the skillet. Add soy sauce and lemon juice and toss to combine.
- Season with salt and pepper to taste.

Nutrition Info (per serving):
- **Calories:** 300
- **Protein:** 30 g
- **Carbohydrates:** 20 g
- **Fiber:** 5 g
- **Sugar:** 8 g
- **Fat:** 12 g
- **Saturated Fat:** 2 g

CHAPTER 5 :
BRUSCHETTA

BRUSCHETTA WITH COD LIVER

Servings: 2
Prep Time: 15 minutes
Cook Time: 10 minutes

Ingredients:

- 4 slices of whole-grain or sourdough bread
- 1 can (3.5 oz or 100 g) cod liver in olive oil, drained
- 1 clove garlic, peeled
- 1 tablespoon capers, drained
- 1 tablespoon fresh parsley, chopped
- 1 tablespoon lemon juice
- 1 tablespoon extra-virgin olive oil
- Salt and pepper to taste
- Lemon zest for garnish (optional)

Directions:

1. Prepare the Bread:

- Preheat oven to 375°F (190°C) or use a toaster.
- Place bread slices on a baking sheet and toast in the oven for 5-10 minutes or until crispy and golden brown. Also, you can toast them in a toaster or grill pan for an alternative.

Prepare the Topping:

- In a small bowl, flake the cod liver into bite-sized pieces.

- Add capers, chopped parsley, lemon juice, and olive oil. Gently mix to combine. Season with salt and pepper to taste.

Assemble the Bruschetta:
- To add a hint of garlic taste, rub the clove of garlic over the pieces of toast.
- Spoon the cod liver mixture evenly over the toasted bread slices.

Serve:
- If favored, garnish with lemon zest and serve right away.

Nutrition Info (per serving, 2 slices of bruschetta):
- **Calories:** 250
- **Protein:** 10 g
- **Carbohydrates:** 20 g
- **Fiber:** 2 g
- **Sugar:** 2 g
- **Fat:** 15 g
- **Saturated Fat:** 2 g

BRUSCHETTA WITH TOMATOES AND MOZZARELLA

Servings: 2
Prep Time: 15 minutes
Cook Time: 5 minutes

Ingredients:

- 4 slices of whole-grain or sourdough bread
- 1 cup (150 g) cherry tomatoes, halved
- 1/2 cup (75 g) fresh mozzarella, sliced or torn into pieces
- 2 tablespoons extra-virgin olive oil
- 1 tablespoon balsamic vinegar
- 1 clove garlic, peeled
- 1 tablespoon fresh basil, chopped
- Salt and pepper to taste

Directions:

1. Prepare the Bread:
- Preheat oven to 375°F (190°C) or use a toaster.
- Arrange the bread pieces on a baking pan and toast them for approximately five minutes or until they turn golden brown and crispy. As an alternative, you might toast them on a grill pan or toaster.

2. Prepare the Topping:
- Mix cherry tomatoes with olive oil, balsamic vinegar, salt, and pepper in a bowl. Toss to coat.
- Add fresh basil and mix gently.

3. Assemble the Bruschetta:
- To add a hint of garlic taste, rub the clove of garlic over the toast pieces.
- Spoon the tomato mixture evenly over the toasted bread slices.
- Top each slice with pieces of fresh mozzarella.

4. Serve:
- Serve while the bread is warm and the mozzarella slightly melty.

Nutrition Info (per serving, 2 slices of bruschetta):
- **Calories:** 250
- **Protein:** 10 g
- **Carbohydrates:** 25 g
- **Fiber:** 3 g
- **Sugar:** 4 g
- **Fat:** 14 g
- **Saturated Fat:** 6 g

BRUSCHETTA WITH SUN-DRIED TOMATOES

Servings: 2
Prep Time: 10 minutes
Cook Time: 5 minutes

Ingredients:

- 4 slices of whole-grain or sourdough bread
- 1/2 cup (75 g) sun-dried tomatoes, finely chopped
- 1 clove garlic, peeled
- 2 tablespoons extra-virgin olive oil
- 1 tablespoon balsamic vinegar
- One tablespoon fresh basil, chopped (or 1 teaspoon dried basil)
- 1/4 cup (30 g) of optionally grated Parmesan cheese
- Salt and pepper to taste

Directions:

1. Prepare the Bread:

- Preheat oven to 375°F (190°C) or use a toaster.
- Lay the bread pieces on a baking pan and toast them for approximately five minutes or until they turn golden brown and crispy. As an alternative, you might toast them on a grill pan or toaster.

2. Prepare the Topping:

- In a bowl, combine sun-dried tomatoes, balsamic vinegar, olive oil, fresh basil, salt, and pepper. If using, add grated Parmesan cheese and mix well.

3. Assemble the Bruschetta:

- To add a hint of garlic taste, rub the clove of garlic over the toast pieces.
- Spoon the sun-dried tomato mixture evenly over the toasted bread slices.

4. Serve:

- Serve while the bread is still warm and the topping is flavorful.

Nutrition Info (per serving, 2 slices of bruschetta):

- **Calories:** 280
- **Protein:** 8 g
- **Carbohydrates:** 30 g
- **Fiber:** 3 g
- **Sugar:** 5 g
- **Fat:** 15 g
- **Saturated Fat:** 3 g

BRUSCHETTA WITH SALMON AND AVOCADO

Servings: 2
Prep Time: 10 minutes
Cook Time: 5 minutes

Ingredients:

- 4 slices of whole-grain or sourdough bread
- 1 ripe avocado
- 2 ounces (60 g) smoked salmon
- 1 tablespoon lemon juice
- 1 tablespoon extra-virgin olive oil
- 1 clove garlic, peeled
- One tablespoon chopped fresh dill (or a single teaspoon of dried dill)
- Salt and pepper to taste
- Optional: Capers or thinly sliced red onion for garnish

Directions:

1. Prepare the Bread:

- Preheat oven to 375°F (190°C) or use a toaster.
- Arrange the bread pieces on a baking pan and toast them for approximately five minutes or until they turn golden brown and crispy. As an alternative, you might toast them on a grill pan or toaster.

2. Prepare the Avocado Spread:
- Cut the avocado in half while the bread is toasting, remove the pit, and scoop the flesh into a bowl.
- Using a fork, mash the avocado and add the olive oil, lemon juice, salt, and pepper to taste.

3. Assemble the Bruschetta:
- To add a hint of garlic taste, rub the clove of garlic over the toast pieces.
- Spread the mashed avocado evenly over the toasted bread slices.
- Place smoked salmon chunks on top of each slice.

4. Garnish and Serve:
- Garnish with chopped dill and optional capers or thinly sliced red onion if desired.
- Serve immediately.

Nutrition Info (per serving, 2 slices of bruschetta):
- **Calories:** 320
- **Protein:** 10 g
- **Carbohydrates:** 25 g
- **Fiber:** 7 g
- **Sugar:** 2 g
- **Fat:** 20 g
- **Saturated Fat:** 3 g

BRUSCHETTA WITH BURRATA AND MUSHROOMS

Servings: 2
Prep Time: 15 minutes
Cook Time: 10 minutes

Ingredients:

- 4 slices of whole-grain or sourdough bread
- 1 cup (150 g) mushrooms, sliced (such as cremini or button mushrooms)
- 1 tablespoon olive oil
- 1 clove garlic, minced
- one teaspoon of dried thyme or 1 tablespoon minced fresh thyme
- 4 ounces (115 g) burrata cheese
- 1 tablespoon balsamic glaze (or balsamic vinegar)
- Salt and pepper to taste
- Optional: Fresh basil for garnish

Directions:

1. Prepare the Bread:

- Preheat oven to 375°F (190°C) or use a toaster.
- Arrange the bread pieces on a baking pan and toast them for approximately five minutes or until they turn golden brown and crispy. As an alternative, you might toast them on a grill pan or toaster.

2. Cook the Mushrooms:

- Heat the olive oil in a pan over medium heat while the bread is browning.
- Add minced garlic and cook for 1 minute until fragrant.
- Cook the chopped mushrooms with the thyme for five to seven minutes or until they are soft and starting to brown. Season with salt and pepper to taste.

3. Assemble the Bruschetta:

- Rub the toasted bread slices with a bit of extra garlic if desired.
- Spoon the sautéed mushrooms evenly over the toasted bread slices.
- Tear the burrata cheese into pieces and place on top of the mushrooms.

4. Garnish and Serve:

- Drizzle with balsamic glaze or balsamic vinegar.
- Garnish with fresh basil if desired.
- Serve immediately.

Nutrition Info (per serving, 2 slices of bruschetta):

- **Calories:** 350
- **Protein:** 15 g
- **Carbohydrates:** 30 g
- **Fiber:** 4 g
- **Sugar:** 5 g
- **Fat:** 20 g
- **Saturated Fat:** 8 g

BRUSCHETTA WITH AVOCADO, PEAR, AND SUN-DRIED TOMATOES

Servings: 2
Prep Time: 15 minutes
Cook Time: 5 minutes

Ingredients:

- 4 slices of whole-grain or sourdough bread
- 1 ripe avocado
- 1 ripe pear, thinly sliced
- 1/4 cup (35 g) sun-dried tomatoes, chopped
- 1 tablespoon extra-virgin olive oil
- 1 tablespoon balsamic vinegar
- A single tablespoon of chopped fresh basil (or a single teaspoon of dried basil).
- 1 clove garlic, peeled
- Salt and pepper to taste

Directions:

1. Prepare the Bread:

- Preheat oven to 375°F (190°C) or use a toaster.
- Arrange the bread pieces on a baking pan and toast them for approximately five minutes or until they turn golden brown and crispy. As an alternative, you might toast them on a grill pan or toaster.

2. Prepare the Topping:

- Cut the avocado in half while the bread is toasting, remove the pit, and scoop the flesh into a bowl.
- Utilizing a fork, mash the avocado and include 1 tablespoon of olive oil, salt, and pepper according to taste.
- Toss the sun-dried tomatoes with balsamic vinegar and chopped basil in a small bowl.

3. Assemble the Bruschetta:

- To add a hint of garlic taste, rub the toasted bread pieces with the garlic clove. Spread the mashed avocado evenly over the toasted bread slices.
- Arrange pear slices on top of the avocado spread.
- Spoon the sun-dried tomato mixture over the pear slices.

4. Serve:

- Serve immediately for the best flavor.

Nutrition Info (per serving, 2 slices of bruschetta):

- **Calories:** 320
- **Protein:** 6 g
- **Carbohydrates:** 35 g
- **Fiber:** 7 g
- **Sugar:** 10 g
- **Fat:** 18 g
- **Saturated Fat:** 3 g

BRUSCHETTA WITH AVOCADO AND SHRIMP

Servings: 2
Prep Time: 15 minutes
Cook Time: 10 minutes

Ingredients:

- 4 slices of whole-grain or sourdough bread
- 1 ripe avocado
- 1/2 pound (225 g) shrimp, peeled and deveined
- 1 tablespoon olive oil
- 1 clove garlic, minced
- 1 tablespoon fresh lemon juice
- 1 tablespoon fresh parsley, chopped
- Salt and pepper
- Red pepper flakes are optional for added spiciness.

Directions:

1. Prepare the Bread:
- Preheat oven to 375°F (190°C) or use a toaster.
- Place bread slices on a baking sheet and toast in the oven for about 5 minutes or until crispy and golden brown.

2. Cook the Shrimp:
- Heat the olive oil in a pan over a medium-high temperature.
- Add the garlic you have minced and simmer, stirring, for 1 minute or until fragrant.

- Add the shrimp to the skillet and cook for 2 to 3 minutes on each side or until they are pink and opaque. Take off the heat.
- Combine lemon juice, chopped parsley, salt, and pepper with the cooked shrimp. If you enjoy a little spice, add some red pepper flakes.

3. Prepare the Avocado Spread:
- While the shrimp are cooking, cut the avocado in half, remove the pit, and spoon the meat into a dish.
- Mash the avocado using a fork and sprinkle some salt and pepper on top.

4. Assemble the Bruschetta:
- Rub the toasted bread slices with a bit of extra garlic if desired.
- Spread the mashed avocado evenly over the toasted bread slices.
- Top each slice with the cooked shrimp.

5. Serve:
- For the finest flavor and texture, serve right away.

Nutrition Info (per serving, 2 slices of bruschetta):
- **Calories:** 300
- **Protein:** 18 g
- **Carbohydrates:** 25 g
- **Fiber:** 6 g
- **Sugar:** 2 g
- **Fat:** 15 g
- **Saturated Fat:** 2 g

BRUSCHETTA WITH STRACCIATELLA

Servings: 2
Prep Time: 10 minutes
Cook Time: 5 minutes

Ingredients:

- 4 slices of whole-grain or sourdough bread
- 4 ounces (115 g) stracciatella cheese (or burrata as a substitute)
- 1 cup (150 g) cherry tomatoes, halved
- 1 tablespoon extra-virgin olive oil
- 1 tablespoon balsamic vinegar
- 1 clove garlic, peeled
- One tablespoon chopped fresh basil (or one teaspoon dried basil).
- Salt and pepper to taste
- For further spiciness, consider adding 1/2 teaspoon of red pepper flakes.

Directions:

1. Prepare the Bread:

- Preheat oven to 375°F (190°C) or use a toaster.
- Arrange the bread pieces on a baking pan and toast them for approximately five minutes or until they turn golden brown and crispy. As an alternative, you might toast them on a grill pan or toaster.

2. Prepare the Tomato Topping:

- In a bowl, combine cherry tomatoes with olive oil, balsamic vinegar, salt, pepper, and red pepper flakes (if using). Toss to coat and set aside.

3. Assemble the Bruschetta:

- To add a hint of garlic taste, rub the clove of garlic over the toast parts.
- Spoon the tomato mixture evenly over the toasted bread slices.
- Tear the stracciatella cheese into pieces and place on top of the tomatoes.

4. Garnish and Serve:

- Garnish with chopped basil.
- Serve right away while the cheese is still creamy and the bread is still warm.

Nutrition Info (per serving, 2 slices of bruschetta):

- **Calories:** 320
- **Protein:** 12 g
- **Carbohydrates:** 30 g
- **Fiber:** 3 g
- **Sugar:** 5 g
- **Fat:** 18 g
- **Saturated Fat:** 8 g

Made in the USA
Las Vegas, NV
05 December 2024

13415196R10063